2/15

D1271461

XTREME INSECTS

Bees & Wasps

BY S.L. HAMILTON

A&D Xtreme
An imprint of Abdo Publishing | www.abdopublishing.com

Visit us at
www.abdopublishing.com

Published by Abdo Publishing Company, a division of ABDO, PO Box 398166, Minneapolis, MN 55439. Copyright ©2015 by Abdo Consulting Group, Inc. International copyrights reserved in all countries. No part of this book may be reproduced in any form without written permission from the publisher. A&D Xtreme™ is a trademark and logo of Abdo Publishing Company.

Printed in the United States of America, North Mankato, Minnesota.
102014
012015

Editor: John Hamilton
Graphic Design: Sue Hamilton
Cover Design: Sue Hamilton
Cover Photo: Corbis
Interior Photos: Corbis-pgs 9, 10-11, 16-17 & 22-23; Hock Ping Guek-pg 21; iStock-pgs 1, 2-3, 4, 5, 6, 7, 12, 12 (inset), 15 (inset), 29 & 32; Minden Pictures-pgs 13, 13 (inset), 18-19 & 24-25; Science Source-pgs 8, 14-15, 19 (inset), 20 & 26.

Websites
To learn more about Xtreme Insects, visit: booklinks.abdopublishing.com
These links are routinely monitored and updated to provide the most current information available.

Library of Congress Control Number: 2014944881

Cataloging-in-Publication Data

Hamilton, S.L.
  Bees & wasps / S.L. Hamilton.
    p. cm. -- (Xtreme insects)
ISBN 978-1-62403-687-3 (lib. bdg.)
Includes index.
1. Bees--Juvenile literature. 2. Wasps--Juvenile literature. I. Title.
595.79/9--dc23

                                        2014944881

Contents

Bees & Wasps

Bees and wasps are both feared and loved. People love to eat sweet honey. Beeswax is used to make candles, lotions, and hundreds of other products. Bees and some wasps pollinate crops. Wasps eat insect pests that invade farm fields and destroy crops.

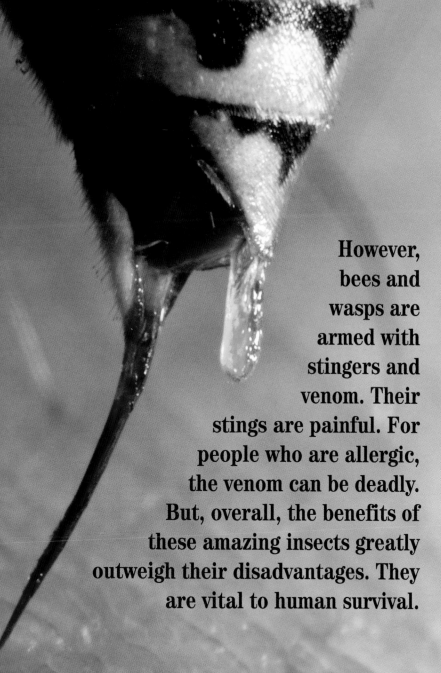

However, bees and wasps are armed with stingers and venom. Their stings are painful. For people who are allergic, the venom can be deadly. But, overall, the benefits of these amazing insects greatly outweigh their disadvantages. They are vital to human survival.

Body Parts

Bees and wasps, like all insects, have six legs and three distinct body parts: head, thorax, and abdomen.

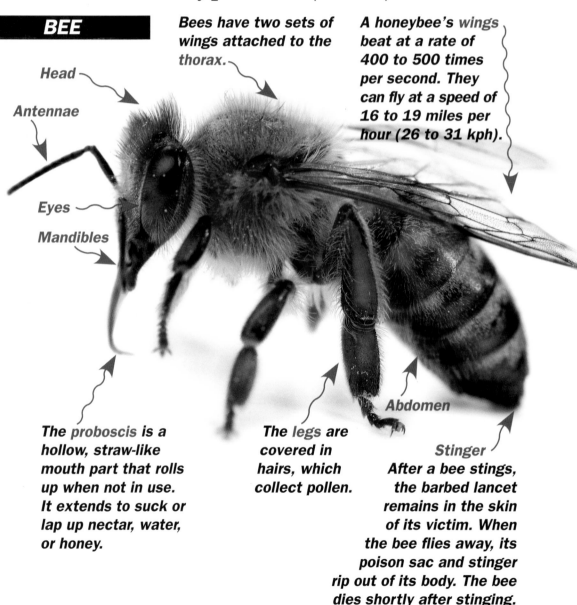

BEE

Head

Antennae

Eyes

Mandibles

Bees have two sets of wings attached to the thorax.

A honeybee's wings beat at a rate of 400 to 500 times per second. They can fly at a speed of 16 to 19 miles per hour (26 to 31 kph).

Abdomen

Stinger

The proboscis is a hollow, straw-like mouth part that rolls up when not in use. It extends to suck or lap up nectar, water, or honey.

The legs are covered in hairs, which collect pollen.

After a bee stings, the barbed lancet remains in the skin of its victim. When the bee flies away, its poison sac and stinger rip out of its body. The bee dies shortly after stinging.

Although they look similar to bees, wasps have a slimmer frame, a narrower waist, thinner legs, and a shiny, often hairless body. They are shaped to hunt for food, not forage. Their stingers are not barbed like their bee cousins. They are able to sting, withdraw, and sting again, over and over.

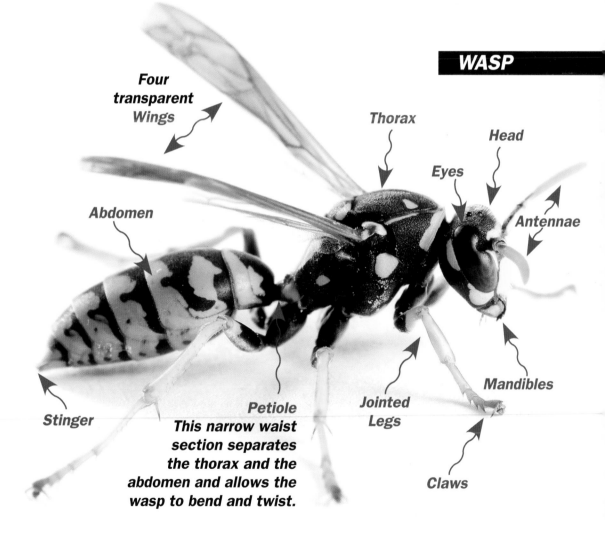

WASP

Four transparent Wings

Thorax

Head

Eyes

Antennae

Abdomen

Mandibles

Stinger

Petiole
This narrow waist section separates the thorax and the abdomen and allows the wasp to bend and twist.

Jointed Legs

Claws

Honeybee

Honeybees are led by a single queen. They are social insects, living in huge groups of 50,000 to 60,000. The hive is usually built in a hollow tree or among rocks. All bees have specific jobs. Drones are male bees that mate with the queen and then die. They have short lives. There are only a couple hundred drones in the colony.

XTREME FACT—The honeybee is the only insect that produces a food eaten by people. They are also very important pollinators of plants. However, many bees are dying for unexplained reasons. This Colony Collapse Disorder is serious. Scientists are working to discover the causes and save the bees.

Queen

Drone

Most of the hive is filled with workers. These female bees do everything from taking care of eggs and infant bees (larvae), to building and cleaning the hive. Workers secrete wax from their bodies and use it to build honeycombs.

Queen

Workers

Bumblebee

Bumblebees live in colonies of 30 to 400 bees. The queen bumblebee hibernates during the winter and starts a new nest each year.

XTREME FACT – To fly, bumblebees have to warm up their muscles to 86° Fahrenheit (30° C). The movement of their flight muscles is what creates their familiar buzzing sound.

Bumblebees are a vital part of agriculture. They eat the nectar and pollen in flowers. The plants depend on bumblebees for pollination. Bumblebee populations have also been declining in recent years. Pesticides and loss of habitat have killed many bees. This has caused great concern because some plants need bumblebees in order to survive.

Carpenter Bee

Solitary bees do not live in vast hives. Most bees fall into this category. Each female is able to lay eggs and create another generation of bees. Carpenter bees live on their own, although many create nests near one another. Carpenter bees tunnel nests in wood. They do not eat wood, but chew it to create walls inside their tunnels.

Leafcutter Bee

A cutaway view of a leafcutter larva and pollen in a rolled leaf.

A leafcutter bee creates a nest for each of her offspring. She uses her mandibles to cut off a round piece of leaf, and carries it to a nesting site. The leaf is rolled and one egg plus food in the form of pollen is stored inside. She will lay 35-40 eggs in her two-month lifespan.

Leafcutter bees rarely sting and are excellent plant pollinators.

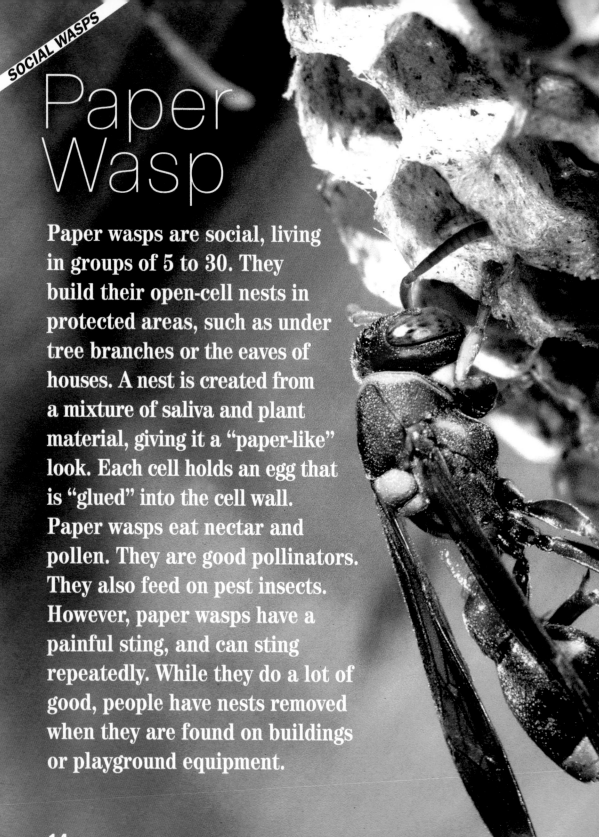

Paper Wasp

Paper wasps are social, living in groups of 5 to 30. They build their open-cell nests in protected areas, such as under tree branches or the eaves of houses. A nest is created from a mixture of saliva and plant material, giving it a "paper-like" look. Each cell holds an egg that is "glued" into the cell wall. Paper wasps eat nectar and pollen. They are good pollinators. They also feed on pest insects. However, paper wasps have a painful sting, and can sting repeatedly. While they do a lot of good, people have nests removed when they are found on buildings or playground equipment.

XTREME FACT – A paper wasp nest hangs from a single stem. It looks like an umbrella. Paper wasps are sometimes called umbrella wasps.

Yellow Jacket

Yellow jackets look like bees, but are ground-dwelling wasps. Thinner and shinier than bees, yellow jackets may live in huge colonies of up to 100,000 wasps. Yellow jackets feed on insects, as well as meat and fish.

A yellow jacket grabs a piece of deer meat to bring back to its young.

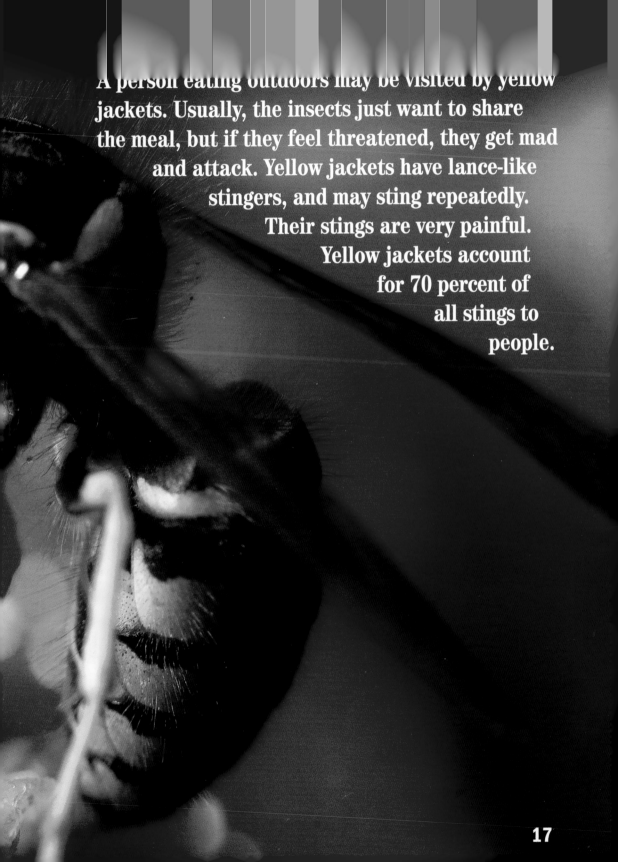

A person eating outdoors may be visited by yellow jackets. Usually, the insects just want to share the meal, but if they feel threatened, they get mad and attack. Yellow jackets have lance-like stingers, and may sting repeatedly. Their stings are very painful. Yellow jackets account for 70 percent of all stings to people.

Bald-Faced Hornet

Bald-faced hornets are the bigger, badder wasp cousins of yellow jackets. They attack anyone who enters their space.

> **XTREME FACT– Bald-faced hornets are also called white-faced hornets or black jackets. The white face (no yellow) gives them their name.**

Bald-faced hornet queens survive the winter and start new nests in the spring. By the end of the season, up to 400 hornets live in their football-shaped paper nests, which hang from trees, utility poles, or even the eaves of houses. Adults eat juices and nectar, but capture and carry insects back for the larvae's food.

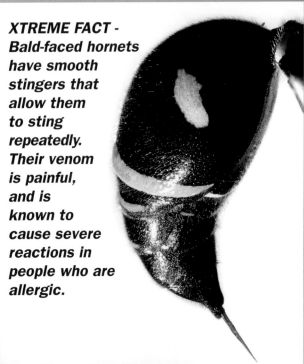

XTREME FACT -
Bald-faced hornets
have smooth
stingers that
allow them
to sting
repeatedly.
Their venom
is painful,
and is
known to
cause severe
reactions in
people who are
allergic.

Velvet Ant

They may look like ants, but velvet ants are actually hairy wasps. The thick, velvety hair may be scarlet, orange, black, white, silver, or gold. Only males have wings. Only females have stingers. Their nickname, "cow killer," refers to the painful sting that is said could kill a cow. However, these wasps are not aggressive, and prefer to flee rather than fight.

Female velvet ant with stinger.

Velvet ants often mate in the air. The male deposits the female near another insect's ground nest, usually a bumblebee or wasp nest in the sand. She lays an egg on whatever pupae or larvae are in the nest. When that egg hatches, the velvet ant larva has a waiting food supply. It eats the other surrounding larvae.

Male velvet ant with wings.

XTREME FACT– Velvet ants squeak when threatened. The sound comes from them rubbing parts of their abdominal segments across one another.

Tarantula Hawk

Tarantula hawk wasps are big and fierce. They use tarantulas for their larvae's food source. These 2-inch (5-cm) -long wasps have a paralyzing venom. Once a tarantula is stung, it is paralyzed in seconds, and remains so for the rest of its life. The tarantula is dragged back to the wasp's nest and slowly eaten until it finally dies.

XTREME FACT– For humans, the tarantula hawk's sting is one of the most painful of any insect. It has been rated as a 4 in the Schmidt Sting Pain Index: "blinding, fierce, and shockingly electric."

Potter Wasp

Potter wasps build mud nests that look like small pots. They create them using a mixture of mud or chewed plants. A potter wasp will usually lay one egg in the nest. To provide food for its future baby, the potter wasp stings and paralyzes its prey. A caterpillar, beetle larva, or spider is brought back to the nest and sealed in. When the potter wasp larva hatches, it eats the still-living prey.

XTREME FACT– It is thought that Native Americans may have designed pots based on potter wasp nests.

Bees & Wasps in Medicine

Although many people fear getting stung by bees and wasps, sometimes these insects can aid humans. Bee venom is used to treat joint pain and arthritis. Raw honey is loaded with antibacterial qualities and can be put on burns and wounds to help prevent infection. Beeswax is mixed with olive oil to treat skin conditions.

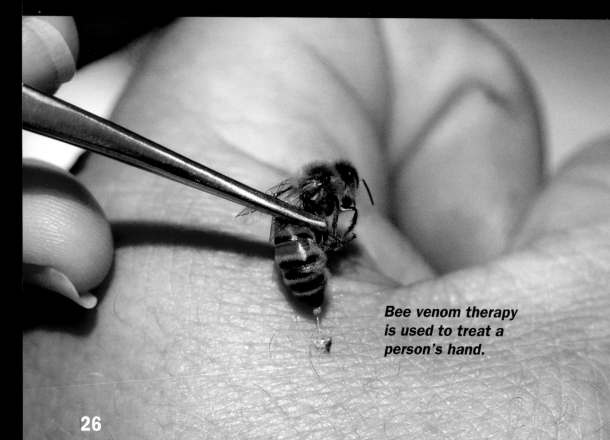

Bee venom therapy is used to treat a person's hand.

A type of medicine is made from the dried honeycomb in hornet nests. The Chinese call it *Lu feng fang.* In Latin, it's called *Nidus Vespae.* People gargle with it to help stop toothaches. It is also used to heal rashes, itches, and sores on the skin. It is not, however, swallowed.

XTREME FACT– Wasp nests are collected when it is cool–either at night or in the fall. Wasps are very protective of their nests and will swarm out to sting intruders.

Can You Eat Them?

Of the people who eat bees or wasps, most eat larvae, the early worm-like stage. In Japan, baby bees are sold in cans. They are called <u>hachinoko</u>. The larvae are cooked in soy sauce and sugar. In Taiwan, people eat fried bees.

Hachinoko

XTREME FACT– Because there is a decline in the world's bee population, it is NOT recommended that they be eaten.

Most people enjoy eating what bees make: honey and bee pollen. These products are usually made by worker honeybees. They collect nectar from flowers and create honey. Pollen is also collected, mixed with honey or nectar, and packed into brood cells. People sometimes harvest pollen granules, which is a protein-rich food.

Pollen
Granules

Honey

Glossary

AGGRESSIVE
Likely to attack, even
without a reason to do so.

ALLERGIC
When a person's body has an extreme
response to a foreign substance entering it. Bee and
wasp venom may cause allergic reactions. Within a few
minutes of being stung, victims experience rashes,
swelling, coughing, difficulty breathing or swallowing,
tightness in the chest, or even a rapid drop in blood
pressure and fainting.

BACTERIA
Single-celled organisms that often cause
illness and disease in humans.

BEE VENOM THERAPY
Allowing live bees to inject their
venom into a human body part in
order to stop pain or cure other
physical problems.

FORAGER
A human or animal who searches in a
wide area for food.

MANDIBLES
Strong, beak-like mouth organs that are used for grabbing and biting food.

POLLINATION
An act where pollen is carried from one flower to another.

SCHMIDT STING PAIN INDEX
A scale that rates the painfulness of stings, ranging from 0 (least painful) to 4 (most painful). It was invented by Justin O. Schmidt, an American entomologist (insect scientist). Common bee stings are rated 2. The tarantula wasp has a pain index of 4, the most painful.

THORAX
The middle section of an insect's body, between the head and the abdomen.

VENOM
A poisonous liquid that some insects and reptiles, such as bees, wasps, and snakes, use for killing prey and for defense.

Index